20/20 Vision

20/20 Vision:

Seeing and Believing What God Says

Dr. Reno I. Johnson

FRESH TOUCH PUBLISHING

Fresh Touch Publishing
www.arjm.org
P. O. Box 162392
Altamonte Springs Fl. 32716

Fresh ! Touch
——PUBLISHING——

© 2020 by Dr. Reno I. Johnson

All rights reserved solely by the author. The author guarantees all contents are original and do not infringe upon the legal rights of any other person or work. No part of this book may be reproduced in any form without the permission of the author. The views expressed in this book are not necessarily those of the publisher.

Unless otherwise indicated, Scripture quotations taken from the King James Version (KJV) – *public domain*.

Printed in the United States of America.

ISBN-13: 978-0-9824-2339-4

Table of Contents

Introduction vii

Chapter One: Seeing What God Says 1

Chapter Two: Believing What God Says 19

Chapter Three: Embracing What God Says 37

Chapter Four: Focusing on What God Says 55

Chapter Five: Afterword. 71

ABOUT THE AUTHOR 77

CONTACT THE AUTHOR 79

Other Books by the Author 81

Introduction

Seeing Well: The Key to Pleasing God

THE GREATEST WORDS any of us could ever hope to hear from Jesus when we finally get to meet Him face to face must be those of the master in the parable He told that is recorded in Matthew 25, "Well done, thou good and faithful servant."

There can surely be nothing more fulfilling than arriving home in heaven knowing we have pleased our Lord and Savior in the way we have lived here on earth. Whether we have achieved what others consider to be great things or lived an outwardly ordinary existence does not matter as long as we have been true to God's unique call on our lives.

But experiencing that incredible welcome—"Good job!"—depends in part on another compliment God pays in the Bible.

"Thou hast seen well."

These words in Jeremiah 1:12 were spoken to the prophet somewhere around 626 BC. Initially, the man chosen to be God's mouthpiece tried to get out of the responsibility. "I'm too young," he argued in the account of his calling found in Jeremiah 1.

But God was having none of it:

"Say not, I am a child," He countered. "For thou shalt go to all that I shall send thee, and whatsoever I command thee thou shalt speak. Be not afraid of their faces: for I am with thee to deliver thee, saith the Lord" (verses 6-8).

In an amazing encounter, God touched Jeremiah's mouth and told him, "See, I have this day set thee over the nations and over the kingdoms, to root out, and to pull down, and to destroy, and to throw down, to build, and to plant" (verse 10).

There wasn't anything for Jeremiah to see literally, of course. God was telling his prophet that while he may not recognize what God was talking about, because He had spoken, it was a settled fact.

Next, when God showed him something, he was asked what it was. "And I said, I see a rod of an almond tree," Jeremiah answered (verse 11).

"Then said the Lord unto me, Thou hast well seen: for I will hasten my word to perform it" (verse 12).

We must see well if we are to do His will well. Our spiritual vision must be 20/20.

Clarity of sight, seeing what God was showing him, would sustain Jeremiah through many years of hardship. Persecuted and ignored, he diligently spoke God's words to the people as a good and faithful servant.

I've faced some hard times in my years of ministry, though nothing like the rejection that Jeremiah faced. But there have been setbacks and disappointments, crises and challenges. What has kept me going has been seeing what God was showing me.

Introduction

The tricky thing is that we can start to lose sight of what He has shown us quite subtly. I first became aware of that when I was in my early thirties. Having read the Bible and studied Christian books from morning to night for years, I realized I was finding it harder to make out some of the smaller print.

Neither of my parents had ever worn spectacles, and my eyesight had always been fine, so it was a surprise to learn that I needed glasses. All that time looking at the pages had taken their toll, but with corrective lenses I was soon able to see clearly again. I now had 20/20 vision once more.

It wasn't a one-time fix, however. I have had to change my prescription as my eyesight has continued to deteriorate a little as I get older. My optometrist explained how, as we age, we tend not to see as sharply as we used to.

This has been an issue not only in my physical life, but spiritually, too. There have been times when I have not seen as clearly as before what God was doing or where He was leading me. I have needed to check and renew my vision.

How about you?

Are you in a place in your life, a season, where you don't see Him as sharply as you once did? You remember how He spoke some things into your life about your purpose and your future. Promises of blessings and fruitfulness. But now, well, it's not so clear.

If that is true, let me encourage you. God wants to restore your sight, just as Jesus touched the eyes of the blind when He walked the earth. He wants to give you 20/20 vision, In the following pages, we'll consider some of the reasons we can lose our clarity of sight, and how

20/20 VISION

with God's help we can find renewed focus—and *see well*: 20/20 vision!

Chapter One

SEEING WHAT GOD SAYS

NO MATTER HOW powerfully God has worked in your life, chances are there have been times—or will be—when your faith started to fade. Even the most spiritually strong have moments or seasons of weakness.

Think of Elijah, a great servant of God if ever there was one. In 1 Kings 18 we read how he single-handedly took on 450 prophets of Baal in a trial by fire—even dousing his own bonfire pile in water before seeing it burst into flames while his opponents' wood remained untouched.

What a miraculous moment. How he must have thrilled to see God in action like that. Yet in the very next chapter we find Elijah running away in fear, then collapsing in despair. His confidence in God seems to have evaporated.

Can you identify? Have found ever yourself wondering where God went, or what happened to the promises He once spoke to you? I know I have.

At times like this, it's comforting and strengthening to hold on to the truths of Scripture. For those who are weary, it can be good to remember the words of Isaiah 40:29-31:

> He giveth power to the faint; and to them that have no might he increaseth strength. Even the youths shall faint and be weary, and the young men shall utterly fall: But they that wait upon the LORD shall renew their strength; they shall mount up with wings as eagles; they shall run, and not be weary; and they shall walk, and not faint.

Those words have refreshed my own soul and brought comfort and new hope to those I have shared them with.

An eagle's wingspan can reach as much as seven feet. Imagine gliding high on those outstretched feathers! But much as I welcome the idea of soaring on eagles' wings, there is another characteristic of those great birds of prey I admire even more: their eyesight.

Normal human vision is said to be 20/20. That means you can see from 20 feet away what the average person can. If you go to the eye doctor like I did and he tells you that you have 20/40 vision, this is not an improvement! It means that what the average person can see from 40 feet, you can only see when you are 20 feet away.

In other words, your vision is dimming.

If 20/20 vision sounds good to you, consider an eagle's. It has 20/5 vision. That means it can see from 20 feet away what you can only see from a distance of five feet.

Three times sharper, four times clearer. No wonder the eagle is such a powerful hunter. It's said that an eagle can spot an ant from ten stories high, or a rabbit from a mile away. It will hang there in the sky, lock in on its prey, and then swoop in for the kill.

Oh, to see things so clearly and surely! If you are feeling a little lost, if the hope you once had is leaking, if you wonder whether God is going to come through as you once believed He would, then I believe you need to have your spiritual eyesight restored.

As you begin to "see well" again, as God spoke to Jeremiah about, you will find your faith being restored and renewed. God wants your spiritual vision to be 20/20.

What happens when we lose clear sight? In place of focus there is fuzziness. Where there was faith there is doubt. Where there was conviction there is uncertainty. Where there was hope there is despondency.

When we lose focus, we end up seeing fuzzy.

Physically and spiritually, there are two main reasons for loss of clear vision—distraction and distortion.

Distraction: Taking your eyes off what matters

Some Christians are critical of technology and its negative impact, but I love the way it can be harnessed for ministry purposes. Jesus managed to communicate to masses with no equipment, but I find it helpful in my church!

However, you have to use technology properly. When we first began using video cameras, they were Panasonic DVX models. These were autofocus, which we thought meant that they would be easy to operate, so pretty much anyone could use them.

But we discovered that the cameras didn't know where to focus. The operator would point the camera at me, but it might try to zero in on the wall behind me. If someone moved behind me, it would jump onto them. And forget it if I were to stand next to someone or even move around in the crowd! We just couldn't maintain the right focus.

The answer was to ditch those autofocus cameras for manual focus JVCs. Now, each time I step to the pulpit, the camera operator zooms in on me and locks his attention. Wherever I move, he tracks with me.

I learned a couple of things from this experience. First, that it is easy to get distracted from what really matters by random movement. We need to learn to pay attention to what really matters and not allow our eyes to be lured away by something bright and shiny that flits across our path.

Our camera problems also reminded me that God's promises are not "automatic." Yes, He will bring to pass what He says, but it doesn't just happen. We get to play a part in seeing that it comes about.

He speaks the word, He sets out the prize, but we have to keep our eyes on it and work towards it, cooperating with God in the process. We have to believe that whatever we find ourselves going through, God will bring about what He said. We must focus on seeing what God says!

The word *focus* means to fix attention on something. Stay locked in on it.

Has God made you any promises? Has God told you that you are going to have a successful ministry? A successful business? That you will travel the world? That you will be married by a certain age? That you will have great success? If so, set your focus on that and don't let anything or anyone distract or detour you. Lock in on it like a heat-seeking missile that tracks down its target.

Seeing What God Says

As the American doctor and writer Oliver Wendell Holmes, Sr. said, "The great thing in this world is not so much where we stand as in what direction we are moving." What are your eyes set on? What is it that you are hoping and trusting God for? You must look to what He has spoken.

After his encounter with the prophets of Baal, Elijah told King Ahab that the drought that had long gripped Samaria was coming to an end soon. He spoke what God had said, and looked for it—sending his servant to peer at the horizon (1 Kings 18:43).

He had to be persistent. It wasn't until his seventh time at the lookout that Elijah's servant saw something, and even then it was only "a little cloud out of the sea, like a man's hand" (verse 44). But before long, there was "a great rain" (verse 45).

If God has said it's there, it is there even if it is not visible to the natural eye as yet. You will have to use your spiritual eyesight like Elijah did. Elijah must have said, "I know what I heard, I know what I see, and I know what He said." He had 20/20 vision!

Looking to what God has said is essential. God told Abraham that He would make him a great nation, and that through him all the nations of the world would be blessed—quite a promise!

But Abraham had to see before he received. In Genesis 12.1, we read, "Now the Lord had said unto Abraham, get thee out of thy country and from thy kindred and from thy father's house unto a land that *I will show thee*" (emphasis added).

When God tells you something, you need to see it first—not necessarily with your physical eyes but with your spiritual eyes, through the eyes of faith. If He tells you He is going to bring you into a broader place, you need to see yourself in that wealthy position.

I'm not saying that we make things happen by our wishful thinking: we are simply agreeing with what God has said, anticipating its fulfillment. But by doing so, we can join Him and "calleth those things which be not as though they were" (Rom. 4:17). Though we don't create the future, there is also an element in which our attitude is important. The words we speak are important, and certainly our actions are important too.

In his book, *Be All You Can Be: A Challenge to Stretch Your God-Given Potential,* author and leadership expert John Maxwell tells the story of going to watch a basketball game and being pumped when the players ran out onto the court and into the spotlight as their names were called, everyone screaming for them.

He envisioned the same thing happening for him. So he went home and started practicing and practicing, finally getting onto a youth league team. One day the team went to the same basketball court where he had first been inspired by the players' grand entrance. He got to run out to applause and cheers—just as he had imagined and envisioned.

John saw something and he went after it!

Sometimes, like for Abraham, the journey to what God has in store can be a long one. If that's your situation, it may help to follow in his steps. As Abram—before God gave him his new name—made his way through Canaan, God spoke and promised to give him the land.

"So he built there an altar unto the Lord" (Gen. 12: 7). In other words, Abram worshiped. He stopped to praise

God, to express his devotion, to offer sacrifices. By doing this, Abram was loudly declaring that "God is not a man, that he should lie... hath he said, and shall he not do it? or hath he spoken, and shall he not make it good?" (Num. 23:19).

By pausing similarly to thank God for His goodness and kindness, and the promises He has made to us, we can stir up our faith. We remind ourselves that He is in control, even if we do not see all that He is doing at the moment. Speaking and singing words of faith can also drown out the whispers of the enemy who wants to come and discourage you and blur your vision.

One time I was facing a financial crunch, with an imminent bill and a family vacation we had been looking forward to coming up soon and needing to be paid for as well.

I went to church that Monday morning and metaphorically built an altar. I told God how good and great He was, and spoke the things He had told me previously, how He had promised to meet my needs. I declared that I was not going to lose focus, I was not going to be knocked off track; that I was going to be steadfast.

Shortly after, one of my staff came and told me that someone was at the door asking to see me. This person came into my office and handed me $4,000 in cash. "Pastor," they said, "I had been keeping this money to go shopping but here it is, right on time for what you need to do."

Learning to focus

There are two ways of thinking about focus. One is that it means knowing what to concentrate on, what to lock your eyes on. The other is that it requires knowing what *not* to look at! As the American philosopher William James said, "The art of being wise is the art of knowing what to overlook."

A wise man ignores his environment. An individual who is focused ignores their problems and focuses on the promises. They don't get sidetracked or sidelined.

Abram faced this challenge on his way to what God had promised him, Genesis 14 recalls. Along the way, Abram's nephew, Lot, is taken into captivity by a group of rebel kings. Abram frees his relative, returning with captives and spoils from those he has defeated.

Then he meets the king of Sodom, who wanting to show his appreciation for what Abram has done, tells him, "Give me the persons, but take the goods for yourself."

But Abram replies, "I have lift up mine hand unto the LORD, the most high God, the possessor of heaven and earth, that I will not take from a thread even to a shoelatchet, and that I will not take any thing that is thine, lest thou shouldest say, I have made Abram rich: Save only that which the young men have eaten, and the portion of the men which went with me, Aner, Eshcol, and Mamre; let them take their portion" (verses 22-24).

It could have been easy for Abram to have kept some of the spoils. He might even have persuaded himself that this was part of the way that God intended to bless him, as He had promised. But he knew this wasn't really the case. Abram did not want anything or anyone other than God to be mistaken for the source of blessing he knew was coming his way.

Perhaps like Abram you need to turn something down because it is not what God really has for you. If you are not completely focused on Him, you may mistakenly see something as part of His blessing when it is really just a distraction.

Note God's confirmation of Abram's decision. After Abram tells the king of Sodom, "Thanks, but no thanks," the word of the Lord comes to him in a vision: "Fear not, Abram: I am thy shield, and thy exceeding great reward" (Gen.15:1).

When we don't hold firm to what God has said, we can find ourselves connecting with the wrong people, and making the wrong decisions. That is why we must stay focused on seeing what God says!

The source of distractions

It's important to recognize that distractions come from different places. You are probably familiar with the saying that the three greatest challenges a Christian faces are from the world, the flesh, and the devil. Well, they are the source of most distractions, too.

The *world* may include those around you. They are not necessarily out to set you back. They could be good friends, or even family members, with your best interests at heart. Because they don't like to see you stuck or struggling, they might suggest what they think is a shortcut to get you to where you want to be quicker. It's just not God's way.

Eliphaz, Bildad, and Zophar come to mind. When their friend, Job, was crushed by all his losses, they came to his side. They wanted to be there for him. Their motives were good, but their words were unhelpful.

Indeed, what they told Job was so off track that God was angry with them: "And it was so, that after the Lord had spoken these words unto Job, the Lord said to

Eliphaz the Temanite, My wrath is kindled against thee, and against thy two friends: for ye have not spoken of me the thing that is right, as my servant Job hath" (Job. 42:7).

After the world, there is the danger of the *flesh*: your own weakness, frustration, or disappointment. You start to look for a way out of or round your present circumstances. You try to persuade yourself that this person or situation that has come into your life is God's way of bringing you to all that He has promised—though, if you're really honest with yourself, you probably know deep down that isn't the case.

Abram found himself in this place. Despite knowing God's promise to him that he would be blessed with descendants, he began to doubt. "And Abram said, Lord GOD, what wilt thou give me, seeing I go childless, and the steward of my house is this Eliezer of Damascus? And Abram said, Behold, to me thou hast given no seed: and, lo, one born in my house is mine heir" (Gen. 15:2-3).

Getting older, the only person Abram can see around is Eliezer, the head of his household staff but not part of his family. He seems defeated, deciding that this must be what God meant. But he is corrected: "And, behold, the word of the LORD came unto him, saying, This shall not be thine heir; but he that shall come forth out of thine own bowels shall be thine heir" (Gen. 15:4).

Take this away from Abram's wavering if you are uncertain about something God has spoken to you of in the past: most likely the thing that you can see near is not what God said. It's close, so you are tempted to settle, to screw up your eyes a bit and convince yourself it's the same as what you have been shown.

Seeing What God Says

It's not hard to fall for a lookalike. Just ask Jacob. He had longed for Rachel throughout the seven hard years he had worked for her father, Laban, to earn her hand in marriage. But Genesis 29 recounts how he wakes up the morning after his wedding night to find not Rachel lying next to him, but her sister Leah. The two shared DNA, family history, maybe even looks. They were similar—but not the same person. Leah was not the right one.

Maybe the lights were low. Perhaps Jacob had drunk a little bit too much celebratory wine. Or maybe he was just so ready for the fulfillment of what he had been waiting for that he ignored a flicker of doubt.

After the world and the flesh, then there's the *devil*. Sometimes the enemy will directly try to interfere in your life, luring you in ways that lead you to take your eyes off what God has said. Don't be distracted!

He will bring something to us to divert or deflect us from what God really has in mind. Sometimes these are seemingly "good things," because the enemy knows it may be easier to trick us this way than to lure us into clear disobedience.

But oftentimes he isn't the initiator: he is content to sit back and for the world or the flesh to do its work—and then he jumps in and tries to further capitalize on the diversion you have welcomed.

Rather than the enemy's doing, it can be our own impatience or weariness. If we have been waiting a long time for the fulfillment of a promise, we can find ourselves starting to look around for something else. We seek relief now rather than riches later.

The trouble is that what you intend to be a short time-out can become a long detour. A temporary fix can keep you from a permanent solution. When we become impatient we are vulnerable to settling for almost anything that looks good or makes us feel good.

Whether the enemy was behind it all or has simply piggybacked on other events, remember that his end game is always to get you to doubt God. It's been that way from the very beginning.

When Satan lured Eve to eat from the forbidden tree of the knowledge of good and evil, she initially resisted by recalling God's prohibition. His response was to tell Eve that God didn't want Adam and Eve to become like Him. He was trying to make her question God's character by doubting His words. He even told her that if she did eat the fruit, "your eyes shall be opened" (Gen. 3:5)—he was telling her she'd see more clearly, when the exact opposite was the truth.

Satan does not want us to see clearly what God has said!

Distortion: Losing your sense of clarity

It's one thing to lose sight of your goal because your attention is caught by something else to which you turn your gaze. It's another to still be looking in the right direction but realize that what's ahead is getting blurry.

There are different reasons that our vision begins to distort. One is age, as I have experienced: our eyes lose their strength and elasticity. We can "harden" spiritually, too, as time goes by and we don't feel we are getting any closer to the fulfillment of what God spoken. We begin to feel disappointed, and allow that to ferment and become resentment, even bitterness.

Seeing What God Says

Poor health is a common cause of impaired eyesight, whether that's due to diabetes or high blood pressure or some other condition. Good diet and exercise are important to reduce these dangers—just as we must guard our spiritual health through reading God's Word, prayer, fasting, consecration, worship, fellowship, and service.

Then there is injury. In the same way that a blow to the head or an infection can damage our vision, so emotional wounds can affect our ability to see well spiritually—maybe someone we trusted lets us down or we are treated unjustly in some way. Untreated, undealt with, hurts and resentments will impede our ability to see and hear God.

Whatever the cause, it's hard to walk confidently ahead when you don't see what you are aiming for clearly. Even worse than blurred vision is double vision—when you don't know which of the two images that are in front of you to aim for.

Maybe the apostle James had that in mind when he wrote:

> If any of you lack wisdom, let him ask of God, that giveth to all men liberally, and upbraideth not; and it shall be given him. But let him ask in faith, nothing wavering. For he that wavereth is like a wave of the sea driven with the wind and tossed. For let not that man think that he shall receive any thing of the Lord. A double minded man is unstable in all his ways.
> - James 1:5-8

You have probably known people like this. One minute they are telling you that God is leading them left, and the next minute they are saying that, no, actually He is taking them right. They have taken their eyes off of what they have seen, and fallen victim to uncertainty.

Keep facing forward
When you stand firm on what God has told you, when you continue to see what He has shown you, you will not look to the left nor to the right. You keep your eyes fixed ahead. You echo the words of the apostle Paul, "Forgetting those things which are behind, and reaching forth unto those things which are before, I press toward the mark for the prize of the high calling of God in Christ Jesus" (Phil. 3:13-14).

I learned this lesson from the world of gambling, believe it or not. When I lived for a time in West Palm Beach, Florida, before I was following God in my life, I would go sometimes to the dog track on Okeechobee Boulevard.

I was fascinated to learn how the greyhounds were so focused, ignoring the lights and the smells and the noise of the crowd, and tearing round that track like their lives depended on it. They were following the lure, a bone running just ahead of them on an extended arm.

They could just see the bone through the starting gate into which they were loaded. Their eyes were fixed on that bone, so when the gun went off and the gates were opened, they were glued to it to the exclusion of everything else. They were running for the prize!

Take to heart the words of direction from the wisest man who ever lived. In Proverbs 4:25-27, King Solomon wrote, "Let thine eyes look right on, and let thine eyelids look straight before thee. Ponder the path of thy feet, and let all thy ways be established. Turn not to the right hand nor to the left: remove thy foot from evil."

In other words, consider where you are going, think about what you are moving towards, and don't make any hasty decisions. Be sure that, wherever you head in life, it is pulling you closer to what you have seen in the far distance, to what God has promised you or shown you.

It is sobering to bear in mind that getting off track isn't important just because it means we will miss what God intends for us. We will end up displeasing Him by turning to evil!

Maybe you have started to find the road signs are a little blurry when you are out driving, or you can't see the computer screen as sharply as you used to. What do you do when you realize that your vision is fading? Like me, you go to get your vision corrected.

We can do the same thing in the spiritual realm. When you realize that you are not seeing what God has said or shown you as clearly as you once did, don't just plow ahead and hope for the best. But don't be brought to a halt by disappointment, either. Don't allow uncertainty and lack of clarity to stop you moving forward entirely. Ask God for help.

He may come to you as He did to Abram, when he was despairing that his servant Eliezer would be the one to inherit everything as Abram still had no heir. In Genesis 15:4-6 we read:

> And, behold, the word of the LORD came unto him, saying, This shall not be thine

heir; but he that shall come forth out of thine own bowels shall be thine heir. And he brought him forth abroad, and said, Look now toward heaven, and tell the stars, if thou be able to number them: and he said unto him, So shall thy seed be.

God renewed Abram's vision by showing him again. He can do the same for us—through His Word, through dreams and visions, through a prophetic word from someone else. There have been times when I became so discouraged that I lost sight of what God had revealed to me. Then, out of nowhere, He brought a dream, a vision, or a word from someone that renewed my vision so that I could see what was ahead once more. I was seeing what God says, again!

Just like He did with Abram, God wants to remind us of the great promises He has made to bring blessing into our lives, not just for ourselves, but so that others may be blessed also.

The pull away from what God has set before us doesn't just come from each side, it can also come from behind. If there is one sure way of not being able to see what is ahead, it's turning our heads 180 degrees and looking the other way! That's why Paul wrote to the Philippians about "forgetting what is behind..."

Remember the Israelites as Moses led them out of slavery in Egypt and toward their Promised Land. After the initial euphoria of the parting of the Red Sea, they began to get fed up with the desert sand.

Into their second month of trekking, they began to complain. Exodus 16:2-4 reads:

Seeing What God Says

And the whole congregation of the children of Israel murmured against Moses and Aaron in the wilderness: And the children of Israel said unto them, Would to God we had died by the hand of the LORD in the land of Egypt, when we sat by the flesh pots, and when we did eat bread to the full; for ye have brought us forth into this wilderness, to kill this whole assembly with hunger.

God had promised them a land of freedom, flowing with milk and honey, and here they were hankering back after life in bondage, eating only what they were given. Don't fall into the same trap!

A backward glance may encourage you by letting you see how far you have come. It can be faith-building to remind yourself what your life was like and how God has changed you and led you. But don't lock your sights on what was just because things are hard now; turn again to what is to be, to what is ahead.

Focus on the promise that God gave the Israelites when they finally stood poised to enter the land He had ordained for them: "And the Lord shall make thee the head, and not the tail; and thou shalt be above only, and thou shalt not be beneath" (Deut. 28:13).

The Israelites had been given a promise, and God keeps His word. Numbers 23:19 reminds us, "God is not a man, that he should lie; neither the son of man, that he should repent: has he said, and shall he not do it? or has he spoken, and shall he not make it good?"

At the same time, the Israelites' blessing also depended on their doing what God had said, following in the ways that He had shown them—in essence, fixing their eyes on what they had seen of God in the past as they looked to the future.

Join me in moving forward. Fix your eyes on the future, toward what God has promised you. Solomon said in Ecclesiastes 6:9, "Better is the sight of the eyes than the wandering of the desires." Keep focused on developing 20/20 vision!

Chapter Two

BELIEVING WHAT GOD SAYS

LIVING IN A part of the world where we enjoy bright sunshine year-round, I know how important it is to wear sunglasses when I am outside to protect my eyes from the damage that can be caused by ultra-violet light. But seeing well isn't just a result of having healthy eyes, it's connected to our minds as well.

What we see is interpreted in our brains. The images that we register are actually upside down because of the way the light strikes our curved eye, so our brain flips them the other way up so we can make sense of them.

That's just one example of how important our minds are in determining what we see. Now think about how stage hypnotists can make members of the audience act as though things are there that don't actually exist—like the Las Vegas entertainer who has a group of volunteers believe they are jockeys. They become convinced that the chairs they are sitting on are horses, stroking them and getting upset when they are told theirs has broken a leg.

It's funny to watch but it's also a sobering example of the important part the mind plays in what we see, and how we act as a result. Having looked at the ways in which our eyesight can fail us, in the last chapter, I now want to consider how healthy thinking is also necessary if we are to realize all that God has spoken to us about the future.

The word *vision* is defined as the "act or power of anticipating that which will or may come to be," or "an experience in which a personage, thing, or event appears vividly or credibly *to the mind*, although not actually present, often under the influence of a divine or other agency" (emphasis added). This is talking not just about seeing with our physical eyes, but with our spiritual ones—and they are not found in our eye sockets, but in our hearts and minds!

Joseph was certainly under divine influence when he had dreams about his brothers' sheaves of grain bowing down to his in the field, and the sun, moon, and eleven stars bowing down to him. But what he saw in Genesis 37 did not match with the reality of the years that followed: thrown into a pit, sold into slavery, unjustly accused, left to languish in jail. He could have been forgiven for questioning those dreams.

When, much later, his brothers traveled to Egypt to seek help in the famine that had ravaged the region, they did not realize that Pharaoh's right-hand man, to whom they appealed for help, was the brother they had treated so cruelly. But when he saw them, we are told, "Joseph remembered the dreams which he dreamed of them" (Gen. 42:9).

The Bible is silent on this, but I suspect that this was not the first time that Joseph thought back to those dreams. It seems likely to me that remembering them helped him endure the long years of difficulty, so that eventually he was able to tell his brothers, "But as for you, ye thought evil against me; but God meant it unto good, to bring to pass, as it is this day, to save much people alive" (Gen. 50:20). Joseph had seen come to pass all that God said would, and so will you.

The power of memory

Just like Joseph, we need to remember what God has spoken to us. We need to recognize that, in some ways, the key to unlocking our future may be found in our past.

We have to remind ourselves of what God has said. Look back at old journals you may have kept. Reread those notes you might have made in the margins of your Bible. Meditate on those verses you have underlined or highlighted. In addition to this, I have also kept audio files of personal prophecies I have received, and copies of notes I have been sent in which God has spoken to me through others. I go back to them from time to time to refresh my memory and stir my faith.

This has been a lifeline to me at different times. There have been occasions along the way when I have struggled with finances, relationships, and ministry. I've been discouraged by setbacks and challenges, but turning to reminders of what I believe God has spoken has given me the encouragement and inspiration I needed to keep going.

If you feel like your life is in the pits, if it seems like you are locked up, remember Joseph. Don't give up, don't throw in the towel. Remember what God has spoken to you in the past; lock in on it in your mind's eye, like an eagle spotting a fish in the lake below. It may seem like God is on pause, but He has not forgotten you.

In Philippians 1:6 Paul wrote of "Being confident of this very thing, that he which hath begun a good work in you will perform it until the day of Jesus Christ." He was telling them that he knew that God was going to finish what He had started. Are you similarly confident that God is going to finish what He has started in and for you?

Don't forget that "without faith it is impossible to please him: for he that cometh to God must believe that he is, and that he is a rewarder of them that diligently seek him" (Heb. 11:6). In Genesis 15:6 we read of Abram that "he believed in the Lord; and he counted it to him for righteousness."

It doesn't matter how loudly you sing praises in church, it doesn't matter how high you raise your arms in worship or how loudly you speak: if you don't have faith, then God isn't going to be able to do anything for you. You must believe what God says!

This is a bit of a controversial area. I am not saying that we can make God do things because of our faith. He cannot be controlled or ordered about like that. But the Bible is clear that sometimes God only does things because of our faith.

Consider the woman who had struggled with an issue of blood for a dozen years, spending all her money on doctors without results. When she reached out to touch Jesus through the crowd around Him, power went out from Him and she was made well. Luke 18:48 records, "And he said unto her, Daughter, be of good comfort: thy faith hath made thee whole; go in peace."

While Jesus was up on the Mount of Transfiguration with Peter, James, and John, the rest of the disciples were trying without success to minister to a young boy afflicted by an evil spirit. After Jesus had freed the boy from the spirit's grip, the disciples wanted to know why they had been unsuccessful. Because of their lack of faith, we read in Mark 17:20:

> And Jesus said unto them, Because of your unbelief: for verily I say unto you, If ye have faith as a grain of mustard seed, ye shall say unto this mountain, Remove hence to yonder place; and it shall remove; and nothing shall be impossible unto you.

If we want to receive, we have to believe. And we are able to continue to believe even in the face of delays and struggles when we remind ourselves of what God has said in the past, knowing that His word will come to pass one day.

Putting feet to your faith

Faith is defined in the dictionary as "confidence or trust in a person or thing" and "belief that is not based on proof." Both confidence and belief remain abstract concepts until they are acted upon. We have to put them into practice, just like the infirm woman.

She could have been sure to herself all day long that Jesus was able to heal her, but until she stretched out her arm nothing would have happened: she needed to connect with Jesus for His power to be released to and in her.

So how are you demonstrating your faith in what God has spoken? Be cautious here: I am not talking about acting in presumption. We can't be foolhardy and then just expect God to bail us out if things go wrong. But if we are confident that God has spoken something to us, we need to act on it.

When the time came for me to step out into ministry on my own I was excited. I knew that God was leading me, but I did not know how things were going to work out. I started a church with no members—just my wife and our two daughters—and no money.

I knew that I needed a building, so I went looking and found one to rent for $3,500 a month. I sensed God telling me this was the place. So by faith I gave the owner a check for the first and last month's rent, asking him not to deposit it until the end of the week. I didn't tell him that I didn't have the money—and by the time came for him to draw on my check, I did. The $7,000 I needed came in right on time.

Like the woman with the infirmity, I stretched. The disciples stretched when Jesus told them to feed the five thousand with the two fish and five loaves of bread He had blessed. They could see that there was not enough to go round, but they started distributing what was there—though I do wonder whether those who were first to get served got smaller portions!

I suspect the disciples may have gotten more generous with their servings as time went by and they saw that their supply was not running out. Like them, you may need to put hands and feet to your faith!

Lessons from a storm

Perhaps the best single example of stretching is Peter. He and the other disciples were in a boat in a storm when Jesus came to them, walking on the water. Peter said, "Lord, if it is you, command me to come to you on the water" (Matt. 14: 28).

That is a helpful example for us today: don't get out of the boat unless you are sure Jesus has called you! If He is not clearly calling you to do something that defies good sense, you are not exercising faith, you are being pretty stupid! But when He says, "Come," you must respond.

Peter was exercising his faith: he trusted Jesus to make possible what seemed impossible. His actions were a living example of how Paul defines faith in Hebrews 11:1, as "the substance of things hoped for, the evidence of things not seen." Peter knew that Jesus had called him to come, so he trusted Him to make a way where there wasn't one. He literally stepped out.

Dealing with doubt

The rest of the story is important, too. We need to be aware that moments of great faith will be challenged. In the previous chapter, we saw how the prophet Elijah went from being a great man of God, taking on the prophets of Baal in a faith smack-down, to feeling that God had abandoned him, almost overnight.

Peter was out of the boat, walking on water—he was defying the laws of nature! And then he began to sink. Why? Because his vision became fuzzy. Instead of staying focused on Jesus, he started to look at the waves around him. He gave the physical evidence more authority in his life than the spiritual reality. After Jesus had pulled Peter back up out of the water, he asked him, "O thou of little faith, wherefore didst thou doubt?" (Matt. 14:31).

Is He maybe asking you the same question today? Perhaps God has spoken to you about success in business. You developed a business plan, secured some loans, and things started well. But orders are not growing any more, and the invoices are piling up. Things look bleak.

Or is it your marriage? You have believed that God wants to restore and renew your troubled relationship, but your spouse is having none of it. The more you press in to them, the more they seem to pull away. Divorce seems to be moving in like the tide.

Maybe He led you to pursue reconciliation in another broken family relationship, with a child or a parent or a sibling. You prayed, you made yourself vulnerable, and you began to see signs of healing, but they have turned away again for some reason and you don't know why.

Do you feel like you are sinking? If so, stop looking at the waves and put your eyes back on Jesus: He is the one who called you and He is not going to let you drown.

Doubt isn't the same as disbelief. Disbelief keeps faith from ever coming to life. Disbelief was the rest of the disciples still sitting back in the boat. Doubt tries to snuff faith out before it grows too big and strong. Doubt tried to drown Peter's walk of faith.

Doubt comes when our now—our present situation and circumstances—contradicts our then—the future God has shown us. Doubt comes when we don't see how we can get from A to B, and we begin to think or say, "I don't see how God can..." As if we need to be able to imagine or understand what God is going to do for it to be possible!

According to the dictionary, to doubt is to be uncertain about something, to consider it questionable or unlikely. As he walked on the water toward Jesus, Peter became aware of the waves around him and started thinking, "This can't really be happening..." Doubt caused his focus to become fuzzy. He began to question what he knew to be true, that somehow he could walk on water.

The enemy loves to try to keep us from all that God has by getting us to question what we have heard or seen of God. It's been the chief weapon in his arsenal from the beginning. Remember how Satan came to Adam and Eve in the garden of Eden, where they enjoyed intimate fellowship with God.

When he asked Eve about God's instructions for living, she answered that she and Adam had been given access to the fruit of any tree except the one in the middle of the garden. Eating from there would be fatal, she said

"And the serpent said unto the woman, Ye shall not surely die: For God doth know that in the day ye eat thereof, then your eyes shall be opened, and ye shall be as gods, knowing good and evil" (Gen 3:4-5).

In other words, "Did God *really* say...?"

Have you ever heard that question? It may have been whispered somewhere inside you, or even offered audibly by a well-meaning friend.

This is when it is important to be able to go back and compare notes. The enemy is tricky. He doesn't always directly contradict what we may have heard because the contrast between what he has said and what God said is too obvious. Instead he twists the original just enough to take us out. If he can't stop us in our tracks, he will nudge us off course.

Satan tried to use that tactic when he faced Jesus after His forty days in the wilderness. He challenged Jesus to turn stones into bread, to throw himself off the temple, and to bow down by twisting what God had really said in Scripture.

But Jesus was wise to Satan's ways. By going back to what He knew, quoting faithfully what God had actually said, He was able to stand against the temptation.

There are a couple of other lessons for us from this middle-of-the-night storm on the Sea of Galilee.

The first is that sometimes we will find ourselves in situations that are not of our choosing. It's one thing for God to promise some sort of blessing and for us to have to go through challenges to see it come about. That still requires faith, but it can be easier to hang in there when there is something good on the other side. When God leads, it is not always that clear.

We read in Matthew 14:22 that Peter and the other disciples were on the water because Jesus had "constrained" them to get into a boat and head to the other side. The word *constrained* means that He forced them, He compelled them. They were given their marching—okay, their sailing—orders.

The importance of obedience

We need to recognize that there will be times God will tell us to do things that we may not necessarily want to do. However, according to Isaiah 1:19, "If ye be willing and obedient, ye shall eat the good of the land."

Believing What God Says

Obedience is top priority with God. So even the things that He shows us and promises us require total obedience in order for us to receive them. Once we have concluded that God has our best interests at heart we should be quick to do whatever He says, knowing that it will only lead us to our destiny.

Back to the lake: the disciples had just been part of the feeding of the five thousand. Maybe they were tired and wanted to rest. Maybe they were pumped up, and would have liked to have hung around and hear from some of the crowd how amazing they had been. Either way, no doubt their faith was soaring. But then Jesus sent them over to the other side—and left them to it.

Sometime later, when they had been battling the storm for a while, their enthusiasm may well have been starting to fade. I have been out in the middle of the Sea of Galilee—thankfully not in the middle of a storm—and know how wide it is. You can't see the other side even in daylight and good weather. Now it was wet, dark, and windy, and Jesus was nowhere to be seen.

Have you ever been in a similar sort of situation? You have known God's closeness and power recently. Perhaps He has even used you in a miraculous way to touch others' lives and yet now He is—absent. Maybe you feel you are getting close to where He is leading you. And then, suddenly, all hell seems to be breaking lose. Sometimes it's just circumstances. But sometimes it is the enemy, who doesn't want us to be in the place God has for us. In spite of the odds and oppositions, we must still believe every word God says!

Facing up to fear

It's important to remember at times like this that fear not only heightens our senses, it can distort them. After all, when Jesus drew close to the boat, walking on the water, the disciples didn't recognize the person they were intimately familiar with. No, they "were terrified, and said, 'It is a ghost'" (Matt. 14:26).

You have probably heard that FEAR stands for False Evidence Appearing Real. We let what we see dictate what we believe. Don't let your feelings determine your actions. 2 Timothy 1:7 reminds us, "For God hath not given us a spirit of fear; but of power, and of love, and of a sound mind."

Consider this: the very thing that scared the disciples—the rough waves—was the thing Jesus used to come to their aid. What they saw as the source of their death became the source of their deliverance. In the same way, what you see as your problem God may want to use as a platform to reveal His glory.

So, in the midst of your storm, be open to being surprised. Don't let fear cause you to doubt God's ability. Face up to fear and know that God will get you where He sent you!

If, like the disciples out on the lake in the middle of the night, you can stay the course, Jesus will come to you—though it may not be in a way that you recognize at first.

If you feel like you are out in the middle of the Sea of Galilee right now, know that Jesus wants to come to you and tell you, just like He did the disciples, "Take heart; it is I. Do not be afraid" (Matt. 14:27).

Another thing to remember in times like this is the words Jesus had spoken to the disciples earlier that same day. Matthew 14:22 says, "And straightway Jesus constrained his disciples to get into a ship, and *to go before him unto the other side*, while he sent the multitudes away" (emphasis added).

Note that He didn't tell them to *head for* the other side, or to *set out for* the other side. He sent them ahead of Himself *to* the other side—with the implication that their arrival was assured. They would get there—even if doing so might be eventful!

When God sends us out across our own Sea of Galilee, as it were, we may not be able to see the other side with our physical eyes, but we can look to it with our spiritual eyes—with 20/20 vision. We can be confident that there is another side, because the One who created both sides has told us to go. It's about believing what God says!

If we obey Him and start to move in the direction that He has told us, eventually we will see the other side come into view in reality, just as we have seen it spiritually—with 20/20 vision. If it seems like God has disappeared, don't worry. He is not far away. He is watching to see what you will do: will you keep pressing forward, or will you turn around and head back the way you came?

Walking and waiting

One thing is certain: going back is not going to take you forward. Now, when you can't see the way ahead clearly in the physical realm, is the time to hold on to what you have seen with your spiritual eyes, to what God has previously shown or told you. Where has He said that he is taking you? Know that you are going to get there. Let faith be like a radar screen, guiding you through the fog.

Now, if you are out driving and you suddenly hit a thick bank of fog, you would not be wise to keep motoring ahead full-speed. You may want to slow down a little so that you can be sure you don't veer off the road as it unfolds just a few feet ahead of you, and to watch out for potholes or other obstacles. But while you are alert to possible difficulties, you can keep heading in the right direction. No need to take the next exit.

Pilots often "fly blind." They may not be able to register their physical location with their eyes because of their altitude, because of bad weather, or because they are flying through the night. Instead they rely on their instrument panel to tell them they are on the right flight path. At times they will shift to autopilot, trusting that they are locked in on their final destination. They take their hands off the joystick.

We need to do the same. Having set out in faith and with hope in God, we need to trust that He will bring us safely through. There may be some turbulence, but despite the rolls and lurches we are going to make it. Just buckle up and hold on! Before you know it, you will be coming in to land safely.

You may find your faith being stirred and strengthened from an unexpected source. That was the case for Daniel when his refusal to stop praying to God saw him thrown into the lions' den. When Darius the Mede realized that his advisers had tricked him because they wanted to get rid of Daniel, he was disappointed and distressed that he could not rescind the law he had passed.

But as Daniel was being thrown into the lions' den, Darius spoke "and said unto Daniel, Thy God whom thou servest continually, he will deliver thee" (Dan. 6:16). Now

Believing What God Says

Daniel was already a man of great faith, of course, but I believe that hearing this exhortation from the king must have strengthened his own belief in God's power.

Daniel's senses must surely have told him his life was in danger as he found himself among the lions, smelling their scent, hearing their roars, seeing their teeth and claws. But his spirit told him that the same God who had delivered his three friends from the fiery furnace could also bring him through a night with man-eaters. God's got you and His promises are sure. Therefore, you can believe every word He says.

As Martin Luther King, Jr. said, "Faith is taking the first step even when you don't see the whole staircase." It's moving forward, trusting that the next step will be there when your foot lands. We are talking here about what we can't see in the physical realm, of course: but we act because we can "see" it in the spiritual realm—with 20/20 vision. We know that next step is there because God has told us to go that way.

As I have mentioned earlier, that may mean taking some action that demonstrates your faith. For example, when God spoke to me about bringing financial blessing into my life, I took my wife to drive to a neighborhood with larger, nicer homes, so we could picture ourselves living there.

Sometimes moving towards what you believe God has spoken to you, spying out the land as it were, can spur you on in your faith, as it did Joshua and Caleb when they came back from exploring the Promised Land. The other ten spies were discouraged, but not these two.

What might your Promised Land look like? Perhaps you will visit the area you believe God is calling you to live in, as I did. If you believe that God has told you that you're going to be driving a certain kind of nice car, you may want to go and check it out at a dealer's—even ask for a test drive. Don't be hasty, though: there's a difference between demonstrating faith and acting prematurely. Don't be rushed and get talked into buying the new model on bad credit terms.

Walking in faith may mean waiting and not buying a cheaper alternative that you could drive away in today because you know the better option will come to you later. There may be a period of inconvenience between now and then—you may even have to take public transport for a while—but you don't rush into something because you know deep within what God has promised. You hold on by faith, believing what God says!

Simply believing in your heart that God is going to come through for you is not enough, however. James 2:17 says that, "Even so faith, if it hath not works, is dead, being alone." Believing something without acting upon it is meaningless, as the writer of the epistle goes on to spell out in verse 19: "Thou believest that there is one God; thou doest well: the devils also believe, and tremble."

The hard part is the waiting, isn't it? But that's when God is at work. He doesn't just suddenly pull everything together at the last minute, before you step into your blessing. In all that time when everything seems to have gone quiet, He is working behind the scenes, orchestrating situations and circumstances and bringing them together at the right time.

He is like a master chef in the kitchen, watching over a wide variety of pots and produce and making sure they are all ready together at the perfect time to create the most wonderful meal. You are going to be served an amazing fresh-fare dish, not a prepackaged, microwaved plate!

It is like a seed. We put those small things into the earth and then have to let time and nature take their course. But while it's no good coming back each day and digging up what you have sown to check on its progress, neither do you just leave it. You must tend the ground and water what you have sown. You must nurture the seed.

In the same way, we must nurture what we have "seed" with our spiritual eyes, as it were. We need to water and nourish the words God has spoken to us, and also till the ground of our heart in which it has been planted. We need to root out any weeds that might choke what we have planted, or cause it to wither.

One way we nurture this faith is by using our lips. Proverbs 18:21 tells us, "Death and life are in the power of the tongue: and they that love it shall eat the fruit thereof." It can also move mountains, according to Jesus.

When Peter remarked that the fig tree Jesus had cursed the previous day had withered, in Mark 11, Jesus answered (verses 22-23):

> Have faith in God. For verily I say unto you, that whosoever shall say unto this mountain, Be thou removed, and be thou cast into the sea; and shall not doubt in his heart, but shall believe that those things which he saith shall come to pass; he shall have whatsoever he saith.

What might be some of the mountains in your life that need to be cast into the sea, as you boldly speak what God has promised and declared? Are things blocking your way in your finances? In your family? In your health? In your ministry?

All this is not important just to ensure we cooperate with God in seeing His promises come to pass. Exercising faith is not only critical for experiencing God's blessing, it is essential for pleasing Him.

Hebrews 10:38 tells us, "Now the just shall live by faith: but if any man draw back, my soul shall have no pleasure in him." So you might say that faith is not only central to getting what we want from God, but it is also central to God getting what He wants from us. See it, believe it, and you shall have it!

Chapter Three

EMBRACING WHAT GOD SAYS

HAVING A CLEAR picture of what God has ahead for you is critical. Indeed, Proverbs 29:18 cautions, "Where there is no vision, the people perish..." Vision gives us direction and fuel for the journey.

And yet, as important as it is for us to see clearly, there is something that is even more essential if we are to step into all that God intends. And that is to remember that God sees better than we will ever do! This is why we should be all the more willing to embrace what God says.

While the whole thrust of this book is to inspire and equip you to open your spiritual eyes, I also know that we won't always have a clear picture of everything that is going on. At times like this, it may not be because of any failing on our end, but because that's what God has planned.

This is because, at the end of the day, "we walk by faith, not by sight" (2 Cor. 5:7). And what is faith? As we I have noted before, according to Hebrews 11 it is "the substance of things hoped for, the evidence of things *not seen*" (emphasis added).

God wants us to trust and follow Him even when we don't see the end from the beginning, or the middle way through. If everything was laid out in detail ahead of us, we'd be robots not children.

As it is, He wants us to walk in relationship with Him. So sometimes we just have to go on faith, believing that God sees even when we don't. If we don't have that confidence, we can be in danger of our uncertain today making us forget our certain tomorrow.

I have needed to hold on to the vision God has given me at times when I did not see how He was going to bring it about. When I started my first church almost ten years ago, naysayers said it wouldn't last six months. That was not very encouraging! But, as I write this, I have planted three churches, have written books that have blessed many people, and have traveled around the world to proclaim the gospel.

At one stage, I attended a conference in California where someone spoke to me prophetically. He said that God was giving me a preschool through which to bless children and their families. I chose to believe and embrace this even though, naturally, it seemed improbable—the building I'd need that was next door to our church was being used by someone who was very antagonistic toward me and my ministry. No way would they be a part of helping me do something for God.

Still, I held on to what I had been told, picturing little children running around on the property. In time, the people there moved out and I quickly rented the building, paying in advance to secure the premises. It all came from embracing what God said.

Embracing What God Says

This wasn't the end, though. The building remained empty for two years, during which time some questioned what I had done, saying that I had wasted a lot of money. But I knew that God had spoken and was leading me, so I stayed true to my course. Eventually, after three years, we had a growing preschool serving more than fifty kids. Remember that God sees better than you do!

I held onto the vision because I knew what God had said, even though I could not see it at the time. This reminds me of another recent experience, when my daughter Ranae dropped me at the airport for an early morning flight. When I got to the counter, I discovered I had left my wallet at home, along with my identification.

I called Ranae on her cell phone as she was driving back home and asked her to go and retrieve my wallet as quickly as possible so that I didn't miss the flight. I told her it was under the dresser, on the left side, but when she got back home and searched she could not find it. She called to tell me she didn't see it.

This was difficult, because I knew without a shadow of a doubt that it was there. I told her again where to look. "Oh, I thought you said the top of the dresser, not the bottom," she said. Looking again, she found my wallet, and was able to bring it to me in time for me to make my flight.

Ranae looked but did not see, while I knew all along it was there—because I put it there. God sees better than us: if He says something is there for you, it is there! Even if you don't see it. You just need to keep looking confidently. Jesus said as much in Matthew 7:7, "Ask, and it will be given you; seek, and ye will find; knock, and it shall be opened unto you."

Sadly, too many people give up because things don't go their way quickly enough. They stop praying, they stop fasting, they stop attending church, and they stop pursuing their destiny, because they are discouraged.

We must remain disciplined regardless of the delays or the demands. Doing so requires understanding three things.

Understand your process

The good news is that everything God has promised and spoken concerning you is going to come to pass—in His time. If God said that you are going to succeed, then you are going to flourish: see it, believe it, and embrace it.

However, it probably isn't going to come easy. Not just because the enemy is dead set against you becoming all that God intends. It's also because God knows that before you can go high, you need to go low; you need a solid base. A tall building needs a firm foundation. A big tree needs to have deep roots. Without developing endurance, you won't have what it takes to handle all He wants to give. You are not going to make it to the top until you have learned to be content at the bottom.

Remember how, in Genesis 37, Joseph had a dream in which he saw the sun, the moon, and the eleven stars bowing down to him. Soon after, all hell broke loose. First his brothers sold him into slavery. Then when things seemed to be on an upward trend in Egypt, he was falsely accused by Potiphar's wife and thrown into prison. One step forward, two steps back.

David had a similar experience. Not long after being anointed king, he found himself on the run from Saul. In fact, many times in the Bible, those promised by God went down before they came up into the fulfillment of those things. This shouldn't really surprise us. Whenever God is doing something big, He starts with someone or something small. A mustard seed. Two fish and five loaves of bread. A shepherd boy. A baby in a manger.

And in nature we see a similar process. Speaking ahead of His own death and resurrection, Jesus said, "Verily, verily I say unto you, except a corn of wheat fall into the ground and die, it abideth alone; but if it die, it bringeth forth much fruit" (John 12:24).

So don't be surprised if you find yourself facing apparent setbacks. When God makes you a promise, He then has to process you. If you are not adequately prepared for what is coming, you either won't be strong or skilled enough to handle it. You may lose it, or you may treat it carelessly. You have to go through the purifying fire.

I've seen my share of the flames. God has used each of them to humble me, to grow my faith. Don't you let the flames cause you to refrain from embracing what God has said: understand the process!

God has a fire for each of us, tailored to just what we need. He knows what has to be burned away and what needs to be purified. He uses this period to strip us of things—bad attitudes and poor habits—and shape our characters, and to grow our faith and trust in Him.

Having this perspective can help you face every challenge and obstacle that comes your way. That financial challenge, that relationship challenge, that difficult boss, that problematic co-worker, that awkward neighbor, that draining relative, and that ferocious enemy—they may just be something or someone God wants to use to refine you. Welcome them as a blessing—even if they do come in a heavy disguise!

One important thing to keep in mind is that your fire will be different from my fire. So don't try to compare your trials or challenges with someone else's. Your fire may destroy me; mine may destroy you. God knows just what heat needs to be applied where, for each of us to be refined for His purposes. Just embrace what God says!

Even Jesus faced a similar passage. Now, He was sinless and so did not need to be purified by fire, of course. But He was empowered by adversity. After being baptized by John in the Jordan, Jesus was led by the Spirit into the wilderness, where He was tempted for forty days by the devil.

During that time, the devil tried to get Him to trade His situation for food and fame, but Jesus resisted by quoting God's Word. And when the devil had finished his temptations, "Jesus returned *in the power of the Spirit* to Galilee" (Luke 4:14, emphasis added). Understand your process!

The key is to walk in God's ways in the face of temptation—temptation to doubt, temptation to take a shortcut, temptation to give up and give in, temptation to soothe your frustrations in ways that displease God.

Remember that "Blessed is the man that walketh not in the counsel of the ungodly, nor standeth in the way of sinners, nor sitteth in the seat of the scornful. But his delight is in the law of the LORD, and on his law doth he meditate day and night" (Ps. 1:1-2).

There is a tremendous promise for those who do this. "He shall be like a tree planted by the rivers of water, that bringeth forth his fruit in his season; his leaf also shall not wither, and whatever he doeth shall prosper" (verse 3). And that leads to the next important principle.

Understand your season

Doing the right thing is important if we are to walk in all that God has for us, of course. But doing the right thing at the right time is an essential part, as well. Just because we feel something needs to happen now doesn't mean that's necessarily the case.

When she is in the final stages of labor, a woman gets an increasing, overwhelming urge to push down and deliver her baby. However, the midwife or doctor who is monitoring everything may urge her to hold back, knowing that the time is not quite right. Too much pressure too soon can endanger both baby and mother. Timing is crucial.

It's the same in the rest of life. We need to work with God's timing—we need to understand the season we are in.

When God asked Jeremiah what he saw, the prophet didn't just say, "A tree." He specifically answered that he saw "a branch of an almond tree" (Jer. 1:11). This was significant, because the almond tree is unusual, in that it is different to other trees. It blossoms in January, when the other trees are locked up in their winter rest. While they are dry and "dead," the almond tree brings forth its flowers and fruit.

God commended Jeremiah for noticing, because He answered, "Thou hast seen well, for I will hasten My word to perform it" (Jer. 1:12). God was saying that the early-blooming almond tree was a picture that He was going to answer sooner rather than later. Understand your season!

Solomon wrote in Ecclesiastes 3:1, "To every thing there is a season..." That includes time to plant and time to harvest, time to build up and time to tear down, time for war and time for peace. If we don't know the season, we can find ourselves at cross purposes with God, rather than cooperating. When we are aware of the season we are in, we know not to fight against the way things are.

Recognizing that there is an order and flow to life helps us to remain calm. It reminds us that what we are presently dealing with will eventually pass away. The seasons have a rhythm and order to them. Sometimes God does override the way things usually work in the physical realm—remember how He instantly turned water into the best vintage wine, in John 3—but not typically.

God doesn't run everything on *kairos* time—His special, opportune time—for us. Often He takes us through *chronos* time—normal, everyday time—because He is using it to prepare us. It's a time for embracing what God says!

Some seasons are more enjoyable than others. Winter is great for ski trips and warm evenings inside by the fire, but it's not so much fun when you're having to do normal life through weeks of freezing weather. For some people, it's not just a downer, it's a disorder. They suffer from SAD, or seasonal disaffective disorder. It's a kind of depression that may need to be treated with light therapy or even medication.

But winter is a necessary part of the earth's cycle. It's a time when trees and plants get their needed rest. Laying dormant is preparation for spring, when they start

Embracing What God Says

to grow again. Summer sees more growth, in preparation for harvest, and then comes fall. This is when trees shed their leaves to conserve water and energy so they can survive the coming winter. It's a cycle, a rhythm.

We cooperate with each of these stages, breaking ground, planting, tending and harvesting at the right time. Ignoring the reality of the season you are in is like swimming against the tide. That can be not only be futile, it can be fatal. Many people drown each year when they get caught in riptides while swimming in the sea. Rather than let the current take them where it will, parallel to shore, they panic. Trying to fight their way straight back to shore, they simply wear themselves out and disappear beneath the waves. It's tragic.

I've made that kind of mistake myself. When the business I had been building so successfully hit hard times, I just doubled-down, tried harder, and invested more. I prayed, I fasted, but I didn't think to consider God's timing and the season that I was in. I just kept going—trying to plant in the midst of winter, as it were.

One of my stores in particular was in bad shape. No matter what I did, it just kept losing money. Eventually I had to use credit to buy the supplies I needed, but even that didn't turn things around. I ended up losing it all, because I didn't understand my season.

Only then did I realize that the challenges I was facing were not from the enemy. It was that the business was not part of God's plan at that time for my life. I came to the point of acknowledging that I could not change my season, only God could do that.

So I let go of everything, and in due time He brought me out of the business world and into full-time ministry.

He used this process to teach me faith and patience, and to direct my path. As Job said in Job 23:10, "But he knoweth the way that I take: when he hath tried me, I shall come forth as gold."

We need to become like farmers, working with the elements and the seasons rather than against them. It's no good trying to plant when the ground is frozen hard, or under a baking hot sun. You don't dig up what you have planted every week, to see how it is doing.

You might want to take some time to meditate on the parable of the sower, recounted in Matthew 13. We read there how the seed, the word of God, fell on different kinds of ground. There was stony ground, there was good ground, there were weeds. The problem was not with the seed: that was all the same. It was the receptivity, the richness of the soil in which it fell, that determined how fruitful the crops were.

Ask God to reveal if there are stones that need to be removed from your life, or weeds that are choking out the seed which need to be pulled up, so that nothing can stop you when your season changes. These are prayers that God is eager to answer.

In Isaiah 55:10 we read:

> For as the rain cometh down and the snow from heaven and returneth not thither but water the earth and maketh it bring forth and bud that it may give seed to the sower and bread to the eater. So shall my word be that go forth out of my mouth. It shall not return unto me void.

Knowing this, we can embrace what God says. We just need to understand our seasons, so that no matter what comes our way, we won't let go, knowing that God's word will never return to Him void. Understand your season! And that leads to the final important principle.

Understand your part

As the parable of the sower illustrates, cooperating with God isn't an entirely passive thing. We don't get to just sit back in a lawn chair with a glass of iced tea and wait for Him to work everything out. We have to play our part in whatever the season requires. Is it time to dig? Then swing that shovel with all your strength. Is it time to harvest? Then be sure to gather in all you can.

One of the keys of accomplishing and being successful in this season is *determination*. The word means "firmness of purpose, a fixed intention or resolution." It's the inner stamina, the resilience, the guts and strength of character to commit to seeing something through.

You have to tell yourself that you are going to keep pushing on in spite of any obstacles that might be put in your way. Remember the saying that, "A winner never quits and a quitter never wins."

Roger Bannister knew all about that. In 1954, the British athlete became the first man in history to run a mile in less than four minutes, but only after several attempts. He said, "The man who can drive himself further once the effort gets painful is the man who will win."

Important as it is, determination isn't enough on its own. Determination is an inner resolve that needs to be worked out in practical ways and that requires *diligence*, which means "constant and earnest effort to accomplish what is undertaken." This is so important. Understand your part!

You have to be consistent if you want to break through anything, if you want to win. The enemy does not like us and he is going to do everything in his power to stop us. The first place he is going to attack you is in your mind. If he can interfere with your thinking, you will never embrace what God says.

This can require what I call selective blindness. That may sound strange, especially in a book that's all about seeing what God says, but there are two parts to that. Yes, we have to focus on what God is saying and showing us. But we also need to choose *not* to see some things.

That means not looking at what the enemy wants you to. Don't let him point out all the problems and headaches. Take your eyes off all that. Close your eyes and keep fighting. What do I mean by that? Stop staring at what the enemy is bringing to your attention. Understand your part!

Instead of brooding on the problems, focus on praising God for who He is, for what He has done before, and what He is going to do, even though you don't see it just yet. Sometimes you have to sing before you see. Understand your part!

In Isaiah 54:1 the prophet told the people:

> Sing, O barren, thou that didst not bear; break forth into singing, and cry aloud, thou that didst not travail with child: for more are the children of the desolate than the children of the married wife, saith the Lord.

Embracing What God Says

He was telling Judah that things were about to change: God was getting ready to turn things around for them, but they had to act as though it was before it came about. He was reminding them that when God makes you a promise it does not matter what condition you are in when the time comes. They had to embrace it, even though they didn't see it, because God saw better than them. Understand your part!

God can and will do the impossible. He will make the childless parents of many. He will take someone from prison and set them over a nation's affairs. I am talking about Joseph, of course, and it wasn't only his record that was against him. So was his race: Joseph was from a nation of shepherds who, according to Genesis 46:33, were "an abomination to the Egyptians." What an unlikely high-ranking public servant—a reminder that God sees better than us, and therefore we can embrace what He says.

Think also about David's unlikely reversal of fortune. He was top of Saul's wanted list, pursued by the king's army, but when the time came for David to be lifted to the position God had promised, those men who had been hunting him now heralded him.

When Solomon wrote about there being a right time for everything, he also declared that God has "made everything beautiful in his time" (Ecc. 3:11). Not some things. *Everything*—in his own, right time. Therefore you can embrace it, even though you don't see it, simply because God said it.

Things may look ugly right now, but there will be a time when you will see their beauty, as God brings them to fruition in His good and best timing. You may feel like saying, "Woah!" right now, but one day it will be, "Wow!"

Praising and worshiping God ushers in His presence, which changes everything. It brings comfort and peace that defies circumstances. And it can also cause God to move on behalf of His children. Therefore, we must do our part!

I think of when Paul and Silas were thrown into prison for preaching the gospel in Philippi. They didn't complain or grumble. Instead they prayed and sang hymns to God when, at midnight, "And suddenly there was a great earthquake, so that the foundations of the prison were shaken; and immediately all the doors were opened, and every one's bonds were loosed" (Acts 16:26).

Not that there is always a quick answer. Remember that Joseph and David each had to wait many years to see the fullness of all they had been promised—enduring hardships and heartaches along the way.

When you decide to focus on and embrace what God is saying over what the enemy is showing you, it may be that the heat seems to get turned up for a while. If so, don't be discouraged—this is actually a good sign! It means that the enemy knows that you have seen, believed, and embraced what God said and so he will try to do everything he can to stop you, before God rewards you. Understand your part!

Be alert, as the apostle Peter cautions in his first letter, because "your adversary the devil, as a roaring lion, walketh about, seeking whom he may devour" (1 Pet. 5:8). But remember that he is going to be sneaky about it.

Chances are that he's not going to come against you when you are feeling your strength, when you are full of faith, joy, and hope. Rather, he will make his move when you are at a low point, when your vision becomes blurred and you begin to let go of what God said.

The enemy does this because he doesn't want your practice of praise to become a habit, knowing that it will keep you strengthened, focused, and full of faith. He'll try to get you worrying about something to knock you off track. When we're distracted we can't see, believe, and embrace what God says. Be wise to his ways, which include tempting us to make mountains out of molehills. The enemy tries to magnify and amplify things, to make them seem bigger and more important than they really are. He will try to trick us into believing things that are not true, like elephants do.

The old saying that "an elephant never forgets" is used typically as a kind of compliment, but this recall is not always a strength for the animal itself. When they are small, circus elephants are held in place by a simple rope tied to a stake driven into the ground. They get so used to being restricted by the tether that when they have become fully grown—and they can get as big as five tons—they stay put. Though they could uproot that stake with a mere flick of their huge limbs, they don't try because they have gotten used to their confines. Their reality is shaped by an untruth.

In the same way, the things the enemy brings against us can't really hold us back. We have to remember that the things he wants us to believe are going to destroy us are actually the tools that God uses to prepare us. Romans 8:28 reminds us that "all things work together for good to them that love God, to them who are the called according to his purpose."

Now, we have a part in that becoming a reality in our lives. We have to be open to God working those things together in and for us. Rather than resisting we should welcome the opportunity to grow our faith, our love, our patience. We have to do our part.

Sometimes, cooperating with God means just being patient and faithful. One time, I went on a missions trip to an impoverished country where conditions were hard. It made me appreciate my life back home so much more. It was oppressively hot, and there were mosquitoes biting us for breakfast, lunch, and dinner. If that wasn't miserable enough, the food we were given to eat was very different to what I was used to. I couldn't force it down. The first evening, I begged off from the meal on the grounds that I was tired. Going to bed hungry seemed like the best alternative.

Hard as it was, I didn't complain outwardly. I tried to make the most of the situation, and give of my best. I preached at several services where people seemed to be blessed by my messages. I was able to pray with people and see God do great things: one family who had been unable to have children later conceived.

Then we were introduced to a family who hosted us with food so good it made me want to lick the plate clean. And after that someone made me a silver ring as a gift to thank me for the message I had shared.

Now, I'm not saying that God will always turn things around this quickly. Nor am I saying that when we serve others we should necessarily expect to be blessed in the way I was. I didn't go there with that intent or motive. But I hope my experience is an encouragement to you to keep serving God faithfully even when it isn't easy; even when you can't see, still embrace what He says, and remember that God sees better than you.

Be thankful, be hopeful, be expectant, even if the circumstances around you don't make such a response seem appropriate. When things don't make any sense, continue to embrace what He says!

Chapter Four

Focusing on What God Says

I FIND IT interesting that Isaiah is known as "the eagle eye prophet" for his ability to see so clearly into the future. In Isaiah 40:31, you may recall, he wrote famously that "they that waiteth on the Lord shall renew their strength; they shall mount up with wings as eagles; they shall run, and not be weary; and shall walk, and not faint."

I wonder if he referenced the eagle because he had in mind that as they hover high in the sky they can see everything stretched out far before them; they can see into the distance. Being aware of what is on the horizon can give you the stamina and endurance to keep going, because you know what is coming.

I have previously written about how much sharper an eagle's vision is than that of a human: four to eight times better than ours. They can see so much more than we do, not just further but wider. In addition to much greater magnification, they have much a far broader field of vision—around three hundred degrees. When an eagle looks at something, it is larger and clearer.

I didn't explain the big reason for this advantage earlier. It's quite simple: an eagle's eyes are proportionately so much bigger than ours. Though the bird is much smaller than the average adult, its eyes are the same size. An eagle weighing about 10 lb. has eyeballs the same size of a human weighing around 200 lb. Why? Because it needs to be able to see well to survive. It needs to be able to see a rabbit up to two miles away because that's its future—its dinner.

In the same way, we need to be able to see well into the distance to survive spiritually. If we cannot focus well on what may be far off, we won't last long.

We also need to be able to adjust our vision quickly. As an eagle plunges from the sky to attack its prey, the muscles in its eyes continuously adjust to help it maintain crucial sharp focus. As the eagle can attain speeds up to 100 mph as it attacks, it has to be able to keep its target in clear sight as it zooms in for the kill.

That's a little like trying to keep an eye on a baseball being thrown at you by one of the fastest pitchers in the game. For most of us, it is just going to be a blur—and quite possibly painful, too! The eagle, meanwhile, is able to make adjustments that keep its target crystal clear.

That is sort of what Solomon was saying when he wrote, "Let thine eyes look right on, and let thine eyelids look straight ahead" (Prov. 4:25). He didn't want them to lose sight of where they were going, or the rules they could not afford to break.

This is why sometimes things take time with God. It is not that He is playing games with us, it is that He cannot bring things to us more quickly than we can keep them in focus.

Focusing On What God Says

If things start happening too quickly for us and we're not able to make the necessary adjustments to keep our vision crystal clear and remain focused, we can easily accept anything on our way to the top. The result: we never ever get there. We end up missing the big things God had in store for us.

When God begins to accelerate us, we must be able to adjust our vision like the eagle, zeroing in on what He has said. We must remain focused. If we are not able to do this, God will move us forward at the speed we can can cope with.

Our spiritual eyes must be sharpened by prayer and fasting, and studying, hearing, and meditating on His Word. This births faith that in turn causes us to see, believe, embrace, and focus on what God is saying.

So may God strengthen our spiritual eyesight! We need eagle eyes so we can see what God is saying, like Elijah. Remember from chapter one that he was the prophet that sent his servant out to scan the horizon in 1 Kings 18:43-45.

Elijah could hear the sound of abundant rain, but when his servant first went out to check, he could see nothing. However, Elijah told him to "go again seven times" and on the seventh time his servant came back and reported, " Behold, there ariseth a little cloud out of the sea, like a man's hand." He could see the first evidence of that which Elijah already heard and seen was coming, even though it was still in the distance.

We need to be able to see into the distance like Elijah, and know that what God said is coming. When you can do that, nothing will shake your faith! You won't throw in the towel when things get hard. You'll be able to look past where you are now, no matter how insignificant it may be, and focus on what God said, because you know that greater is coming.

Here's what the apostle Paul wrote in 1 Corinthians 2:9-10: "But as it is written, eye hath not seen, nor ear heard, neither have entered into the heart of man, the things which God hath prepared for them that love him. But God hath revealed them unto us by his Spirit: for the Spirit searcheth all things, yea, the deep things of God."

We must have 20/20 vision—spiritual vision that is, clear vision, sharp vision—to see and to focus on what God has said.

It's also important that we have a broad range of vision, like the eagle. We must have a wide view of what is happening. That means not putting God in a box, and presuming you know best how He should work things out. God can take things that seem bad to us and make them work for our good.

Take Joseph as an example. Getting sold into slavery in Egypt certainly didn't seem like a great career move, but in due time he ended up running the country and providing relief for his family when they came to escape the famine in Canaan. He was able to tell his brothers, those who had betrayed him, "But as for you, ye thought evil against me; but God meant it unto good, to bring to pass, as it is this day, to save much people alive" (Gen. 50:20).

You need eagle eyes to see into the distance, into the future, beyond the obstacles and the setbacks and the uncertainties. When you are facing difficulties and discouragements, wait upon the Lord and He will renew your strength. You will mount up with the wings of an eagle—and may you see with its eyes when you are there! Let's see the things God shows us larger and more clearly, like the eagle.

Being single-minded

When an eagle spots its prey it locks in like a heat-seeking missile. We need to do the same. When God shows us something that is ahead, off in the distance, we have to stay focused.

To be *single-minded* means "to have or to show a single aim or purpose, to be dedicated, with one aim." Someone who is single-minded is firm and inflexible, not in a dismissive sort of way but in a determined way. They mean what they say and they say what they mean. Their eyes are on the prize—what God has promised them—and they are not letting them drift to anything else.

Another way to put this is *commitment.* A commitment is "a pledge or promise, an obligation that restricts one's freedom of action." In other words, because you are going after *this* you are not interested in *that.* When God shows you the milk and honey that is ahead of you in the Promised Land, you won't settle for anywhere else, no matter how nice it might seem. You are a prisoner to what God has told you.

So stay in your cell! Keep yourself on lock-down—locked into the prison of what God has said. I've visited people in prison who have their date of release written on the wall of their cell. They don't want to know what day it is now; they are focused on that date in front of them. They know that their release, their freedom, is coming. No matter how hard it gets, not matter how they are mistreated, they know that come that day they are walking out into their future.

That's how we must see it too. You may be in a prison now—financially, spiritually, relationally, vocationally, emotionally. You may have good reason to be discouraged, but you need to hold on to the promise that there is a release date coming when God is going to show up big time on your behalf. Keep it in mind, keep it in your vision.

This requires great *patience.* This is not a very popular word in our instant, microwave world! It means "an ability or willingness to suppress restlessness or annoyance when confronted with delay." That means you have to be able to suppress your desire to try something different and to move out of God's timing.

You may feel like walking off that crummy job, walking out of your troubled marriage, walking away from that failing business, or even walking out of that struggling church. But if God hasn't told you to, take a deep breath and hunker down and hang in there. You need to stay right where you are until your God moment. You need to stay focused on what God said!

When you are single-minded you have clarity of vision and purpose. The opposite is confusion, when everything is blurry. One minute you are saying God can and the next you are saying that He can't. You go to the car lot to buy a Beamer and end up with a beater. God promised you a fine prince with a voice like an angel and you end up with a flabby pauper who can't carry a tune in a bucket.

This shouldn't really be surprising. It's just the reality of James 1:8: "A double minded man is unstable in all his ways."

It's important to add one qualifying remark here. Being focused on the future doesn't have to mean ignoring the present. I know some people who have turned down opportunities and responsibilities because they said they were waiting for what God wants to bring them in the future.

We need to be careful not to get so caught up in what's ahead that we miss what is right in front of us. God has a future and a hope for us, as the prophet Jeremiah wrote, but He is also with us in the here and now, blessing and protecting us, and desiring to use us to touch and bless others. Let's not get too spiritual.

It's like waiting on God's call on your life. You may not know yet what He wants you to do in the future—be a teacher or an attorney or a police officer or a stay-at-home mom. But not knowing what He has for you tomorrow doesn't have to stop you living for Him today. Micah 6:8 says, "He hath shewed thee, O man, what is good; and what doth the Lord require of thee, but to do justly, and to love mercy, and to walk humbly with thy God?"

You can be busy doing that today, while waiting on what He showed you for your tomorrow!

Waiting with wisdom

I've mentioned how having a wide view of what God is doing means drawing from examples like those of Joseph. There are more lessons for us from the life of the man who went from privileged son to the pit and prison before getting the promotion that God had told him would come.

Guard your mouth

First, we need to learn to be careful about what we say and to whom. Declaring what God has told us is coming is important, because it exercises our faith. When we speak what God has said we are agreeing with Him, we are positioning ourselves for His promise and His purposes.

But there is a right and a wrong time to speak about what God has shown you. Joseph's dreams of his brothers' sheaves bowing down to his, and the stars bowing down to him, may have been God's promise of what was to come, but telling them as he did provoked their anger and displeasure.

When Joseph was sent to check on his older brothers and see how they were getting on with the sheep they were tending in Shechem, they spotted him coming. Genesis 37:18-20 tells us:

> And when they saw him afar off, even before he came near unto them, they conspired against him to slay him. And they said one to another, Behold, this dreamer cometh. Come now therefore, and let us slay him, and cast him into some pit, and we will say, Some evil beast hath devoured him: and we shall see what will become of his dreams.

You need to be careful who you share what God tells you with, and when and how, because it can bring out the haters, the jealous, and the envious. Guard your mouth!

At the same time, don't be discouraged if you do find yourself dealing with naysayers and doubters and critics. In a strange way, this can also be a confirmation of what God has spoken to you, because the enemy is starting to do all he can to make sure that you never see what God has said.

I am sure that the devil was doing all he could to ensure that what Joseph had seen never came about. Joseph was fortunate, in that God showed him what his future would look like. But for many of us, God spoke something and through the eyes of faith, in spite of the obstacles and oppositions, we have had to bring it into vision. God wants you to see, believe, embrace and focus on what He has said!

Opposition is the enemy's attempt to keep you from what God wants. He wants to shut down what God has said and shown you so that it never becomes a reality. This is where we need to be able to hold on to the vision. When it is dark all around, we need to be able to close our eyes and see clearly in our mind's eye what the Lord has shown us. We need a certainty and a surety that will be an anchor for us as the storms rage and try to sink us.

We must hold on to what we saw and heard then, and not make decisions based on what we hear and see now. If you do that, you are likely to shut down and back up on God. Remember that "we walk by faith, not by sight" (2 Cor. 5:7). As Duke Rohe once said, "Never cut short your waiting with compromise. Simply put, the waiting's not over until the waiting's done."

Sometimes you have to just keep fighting, even when you can't see well. Like the boxer I saw in a fight one time who got caught by a punch that left blood running down his face. When he got back to his corner between rounds, I heard the fighter tell his corner men that he could not see, his vision was blurred. As his coach worked on him, he told the boxer to keep calm and keep fighting, that the blurry vision would pass and in the meantime he just had do what he knew, and stay out of trouble.

The boxer did just that. He went out for the next round, covering and punching, covering and punching, until he could see more clearly again and take the fight to his opponent once more. That's all we can do, sometimes: keep doing what we know to—praying, praising, trusting, waiting, with wisdom.

Just don't throw in the towel! Don't settle for less. You have come too far to stop short of all that God intends for you, now. Remind yourself that one day you are going to wake up and you will have what you saw, if you will only hold on and not give in. Stay focused on what God said!

When Joseph arrived in Dothan, his brothers ganged up on him, stripped him of the coat of many colors that their father had given him as a sign of his favor, and threw him into a pit with no water in it. Joseph could have been forgiven for feeling very sorry for himself at this point, but there is no record of him being so here—or when things took another turn for the bad in Egypt, when he ended up in prison.

Guard your heart

What happened to Joseph in Egypt serves as another warning to us, about how the enemy will try different tactics to keep us from what God has spoken to us. He will try an all-out assault, like the betrayal of Joseph's brothers and his being sold into slavery, in the hopes that we will get bitter and resentful and give up on God. Guard your heart!

When that doesn't work, instead of trying to get you to give up on following in God's way, he may try to convince you that you have reached your destination before you really have. The idea is subtle compromise: to get you to stop before you have fully arrived.

Remember, Joseph arrived in Egypt as a slave, sold to Potiphar, the captain of Pharaoh's guard. Things started to look up. Genesis 39:2-6 tells us:

> And the Lord was with Joseph, and he was a prosperous man; and he was in the house of his master the Egyptian. And his master saw that the Lord was with him, and that the Lord made all that he did to prosper in his hand. And Joseph found grace in his sight, and he served him: and he made him overseer over his house, and all that he had he put into his hand. And it came to pass from the time that he had made him overseer in his house, and over all that he had, that the Lord blessed the Egyptian's house for Joseph's sake; and the blessing of the Lord was upon all that he had in the house, and in the field.

When you have good spiritual sight, you don't become jealous of other people. Joseph made it possible for

Potiphar's house to prosper. The average person would say, "Why am I making all of this money for you? I can do my own thing." Joseph could have become jealous and said, "God is only blessing you because I am here." But he did not complain, he did not murmur. He was committed and conscientious.

Just as signs of opposition should be an encouragement to us, evidence that the enemy is trying to keep us from something, so should signs of God's blessing on those around you. Let them be an encouragement that He is in the neighborhood and He is active—and that you could be next!

It would have been very easy for Joseph to have settled for what seemed like a pretty good gig: right-hand man to one of the most powerful persons in the nation. But that was not what God had spoken. Potiphar's house was not Joseph's final destination, it was not the palace. Stay focused on what God said! Joseph refused to settle—or compromise, when Potiphar's wife threw herself at him.

Let's get real here: if the enemy can't appeal to our jealousy or resentment to get us to compromise, he will appeal to our hungers, our desires, our passions, our lusts. The enemy will dress someone or something up real nice and send them our way to get our eyes off what is in the distance.

Joseph's response to Potiphar's wife reveals his character and commitment:

> But he refused, and said unto his master's wife, Behold, my master wotteth not what is with me in the house, and he hath committed all that he hath to my hand; there

Focusing On What God Says

is none greater in this house than I; neither hath he kept back anything from me but thee, because thou art his wife: how then can I do this great wickedness, and sin against God?
- Gen. 39:8-9

Joseph told the woman, in effect, "I see you, but I don't see you. You are not part of what God has shown me. You may look good, but you are not part of the vision."

When you are going after what God has shown you, there will come a time when you have to tell your flesh no. What's in front of you may look juicy, it may look sweet, but remember that it is not as good as what God has farther ahead of you!

Keep in mind that this attack may not be a one-and-done assault. Potiphar's wife kept after Joseph: "As she spake to Joseph day by day, that he hearkened not unto her, to lie by her, or to be with her" (Gen. 39:10). She kept knocking, and he kept refusing to answer the door.

Then came a day when no one else was in the house and she made a move. "And she caught him by his garment, saying, Lie with me: and he left his garment in her hand, and fled, and got him out" (Gen. 39:12).

This wasn't the first time Joseph had been stripped of his robe! Remember the coat of many colors, a sign of his favor, that had been torn from him by his brothers, ripped and speckled with blood. Now the clothing given to him as Potiphar's main man was taken from him.

Joseph knew that this was just a symbol he was losing; in his actions he was still holding onto the reality that had been promised. He knew that God could and would provide him with a new wardrobe one day! Joseph was intentional; he was focused.

Guard your character

And so we come to the next strategy the enemy may use to try to keep you from your destiny, to get you to lose sight of what God said: false accusations. Sometimes, if people can't get you to compromise, they will set out to destroy you one way or another.

Potiphar's wife falsely accused Joseph of assault, and he ended up in prison. This was another key moment of testing for Joseph. Would he fall into resentment and bitterness? Would he regret having spurned Potiphar's wife, thinking that he might as well have compromised?

The Bible is silent on all this—and I believe that Joseph was, too. I think that he kept quiet, kept focusing on what God had said and shown him all those years before. Genesis 39:21 tells us, "But the Lord was with Joseph, and shewed him mercy, and gave him favour in the sight of the keeper of the prison."

If ever someone illustrated the saying that "you can't keep a good man down," it surely must be Joseph. Going a little further I'll say that *you can't keep a focused man down*. Here he was again, knocked down once more, but still standing up straight and doing the right thing. When you're focused on what God said, it gives you the resilience to face any obstacle. And, once more, his character was rewarded:

> And the keeper of the prison committed to Joseph's hand all the prisoners that were in the prison; and whatsoever they did there,

he was the doer of it. The keeper of the prison looked not to any thing that was under his hand; because the Lord was with him, and that which he did, the Lord made it to prosper.
- Gen. 39:22-23

In due time, of course, Joseph interpreted the dreams of a couple of fellow prisoners, the baker and the butler from Pharaoh's staff, correctly warning that one would die and the other would be reinstated.

Joseph would remain in prison two more years after the butler was freed before he told Pharaoh of the man who might be able to explain what the king's disturbing dream meant. Delighted by Joseph's explanation of the dreams of the fat cows and thin cows, and the fat sheaves and the thin sheaves, Pharaoh declared, "Thou shalt be over my house, and according unto thy word shall all my people be ruled: only in the throne will I be greater than thou" (Gen. 41:40).

Then Pharaoh took a ring from his hand and put it on Joseph's, as a sign of authority, and "arrayed him in vestures of fine linen, and put a gold chain about his neck" (Gen: 41:42). Joseph got to ride in Pharaoh's second chariot, "and they cried before him, Bow the knee: and he made him ruler over all the land of Egypt" (Gen. 41:43).

Joseph passed the test. Through all his trials, he held on to what he had seen, what God had shown him, he remained focused, and in time it came to pass. God used the very things that were intended to be stumbling blocks and turned them into stepping stones.

He kept his eyes on what he had seen, on what God had shown him. He waited on God and was renewed big time. He had 20/20 vision. May you develop the same clarity of vision for what God has said and shown you, and where He wants to take you. May you, like Jeremiah, *see well*!

Chapter Five

AFTERWORD

Your Personal Prescription

HAVING STARTED THIS book with the prophet Jeremiah, looking at how he emphasized the importance of "seeing well" if we are to please God, it's appropriate we return to his writing as we close.

In Jeremiah 5:21 he warned God's people of the danger of becoming "foolish... and without understanding," the kind that "have eyes, and see not."

Jeremiah's caution may have been the inspiration for the old saying, "There's none so blind as those who will not see." In other words, you can't help people understand if they don't want to.

Having shared with you how critical good spiritual vision is if we are to walk into the fullness of the future that God desires for us, I don't want you to miss out by failing to apply what you may have learned.

I believe the lessons I have shared in the previous chapters can help you "see well," but let me also bring some of them together in this short, summary prescription for healthy spiritual vision.

WATCH YOUR HEALTH

Failing eyesight isn't an inevitability. Some people keep their 20/20 vision well into their old age, and the same can be true for you spiritually—your spiritual vision can remain sharp in spite of the long wait, ensuring you continue to see coming to pass all that God has said. It takes more than just good genetics, however.

A healthy spiritual diet is essential. You need to make sure you're consuming the equivalent of fresh fruit and vegetables that provide the nutrition your eyes need: that is the Word of God. Chowing down on fast food every day is not going to do you any good; you need substance.

Are you feeding yourself well, spiritually? That will determine how well you see, believe, embrace, and focus on what God is saying and how you eventually have what He has said.

It is also important to protect your eyes from the elements: you wear safety goggles when you're working with tools and wear sunglasses when you are out in the harshest light of the day. In Psalm 101:3 the writer knew how important it was to guard his sight from injury: "I will set no wicked thing before mine eyes: I hate the work of them that turn aside; it shall not cleave to me."

What are you doing to guard your eyes from dangers? Remember Jesus' words in Matthew 6:22-23:

> The light of the body is the eye: if therefore thine eye be single, thy whole body

shall be full of light. But if thine eye be evil, thy whole body shall be full of darkness. If therefore the light that is in thee be darkness, how great is that darkness!

HAVE A CHECK-UP

The thing about poor vision is that, typically, it sneaks up on us. When a catastrophic injury causes impaired sight it is obvious right away, but usually things get blurry over time. We don't realize that we have begun to squint, because we just get used to things being a little out of focus. So we try to adjust or compensate.

One way to avoid this danger is to have regular checkups. The optometrist will examine your eyeballs and test your ability to read the bottom line on those sight charts. Similarly, it can be helpful to check in with yourself. Take some time out for a mini-retreat on a regular basis to have some alone time with God in prayer, fasting, meditating, and studying His Word. Ask Him how you are doing.

Look back over your journals to remind yourself of what He has said. Consider whether your expectations are as high now as they were before, when He first promised you. This process is a great way to examine your faith, to see whether you still truly believe and are expecting what God has promised you.

You may even want to get some kind of external assessment: ask a loved one or trusted friend to tell you how they think you are doing spiritually. Do they see you still pursuing the things you have told them God has shown you or called you to?

GET CORRECTIVE HELP

If you find you're seeing less than 20/20, you don't have to stay there in the fog! Lasik surgery can restore your physical vision to the way it was. So can God! Whether you're seeing less clearly because of the long wait, deliberate sin, being weighed down by struggles, or through attacks of the enemy, God can cut to the heart of things like a laser and renew your sight.

As David did, you can ask God to, "Restore unto me the joy of thy salvation; and uphold me with thy free spirit" (Ps. 51:12). Perhaps you may want to ask friends to pray that with and for you too.

Or maybe you realize you need some daily help to keep your sight sharp, just as you would put on a pair of spectacles each morning. That could mean being more diligent about a regular devotional time with God, giving space for Him to speak and minister to you, or some kind of accountability relationship with someone to help keep you on track.

You don't have to settle for poor or partial sight. Jesus wants you to see well. Remember the time He came to Bethsaida, where the people brought a blind man and asked Him to heal?

Jesus took the man to one side, spit on His hands and laid them on the man. Then He asked what he could see.

The man looked up and said he saw "men as trees, walking." This was much better than the blindness he had known, but Jesus had more in mind. In Mark 8:25, we read:

Afterword

"After that he put his hands again upon his eyes, and made him look up: and he was restored, and saw every man clearly."

Jesus wants you to see clearly too, to enjoy 20/20 vision! He wants you to see, believe, embrace, and focus on what He has said. You must see all that God has spoken concerning you through the eyes of faith: then God will cause it to manifest here on the earth. He wants to bring it all to pass in your life.

Finally, having all that God has promised you is very exciting, however, it not as exciting and important as having eternal life. If you're not saved and do have a genuine, personal relationship with Jesus Christ today, I urge you to consider giving Him your heart. Only then will you truly be able to start seeing clearly, and experiencing and enjoying the abundant life God has in mind for us all!

ABOUT THE AUTHOR

Apostle Dr. Reno I. Johnson is a man guided by the Holy Spirit; he is an ambassador of Christ, he is a Warrior in the faith, an excellent Teacher of God's Word and a Dynamic, Radical Preacher. In addition, he is an author, who has written many books that have broaden the scope of individuals globally and they have helped to usher lost souls into the Kingdom of God. He is married to Shandaly Johnson and has one son and two daughters.

Apostle Johnson was ordained as a Minister at The Voice of Deliverance Disciple Center Ministries, Nassau Bahamas where he served for over thirteen years. By divine appointment today, the call and power of God is being demonstrated in the life of Apostle Johnson in such an awesome way. His unconditional love for people and passion for God's Word has been a transportation that has taken him throughout The World at large preaching the Good News of the Gospel of Jesus Christ.

Most notably, he is the president and Chief Executive Officer (CEO) of Reno I. Johnson Ministries International. He was consecrated to the Office of an Apostle on Sunday, December 5, 2010. He is also the founding pastor of

Total Life Church, Orlando, Florida and Divine Encounter Ministries International in Nassau, The Bahamas.

Equally important, he has obtained an Associate Degree from New England Institute of Technology- West Palm Beach, Florida. However, upon receiving the call to ministry Apostle Johnson pursued several Biblical Degrees including a Diploma in Biblical Studies from Liberty University (Lynchburg, Virginia), an Associate Degree in Biblical Studies, and also an Honorary Doctorate Degree in Theology from Bethel Christian University, At present, he is pursuing higher academia in Theology.

Apostle Johnson is a highly sought after anointed messenger of God, whose passion is to win souls for Christ, and advance the Kingdom of God. 'Touching people, Transforming lives'

CONTACT THE AUTHOR

You can email the author at renoijohnson@gmail.com or rijmintl@gmail.com

Please visit the author's website for current phone numbers and address.

www.arjm.org

To order any of Apostle Dr. Reno I. Johnson's Ministry Resources, Please visit our website, write or call us Today!

For Speaking Engagements please call or email us Today.

Connect with us on social media!

Don't forget to visit our Website!

Other Books by the Author

www.ingramcontent.com/pod-product-compliance
Lightning Source LLC
Chambersburg PA
CBHW050604300426
44112CB00013B/2066